Animals
on the
Move

written by Jay Dale

photography by Ned Meldrum

This is my gran.

My gran lives on a *farm.*

She looks after lots and lots of *animals.*

2

My gran is a teacher too.

Look!

The animals are hungry.

I help my gran
with the animals.
My little *sister* helps too.
We give the baby *goats*
a drink of *milk.*

6 o'clock

Look!

Gran opens the van.

The animals go into the van.

The *rabbits* go in.

The *chickens* go in.

And the goats go in too.

The animals are on the move!

9 o'clock

We take the animals to a school.

Gran gets the animals out of the van.

I help Gran.

My little sister helps too.

10 o'clock

The animals go into a big pen.

I pet a soft baby rabbit.

My sister pets a rabbit too.

Lots of baby animals are in the pen.

Look!

Here come the children.

They look happy.

11 o'clock

The children look at Gran.
Gran is a good teacher.

Next the children pet the animals.

A boy gives a goat a drink of milk.

A girl gives a *lamb* a drink of milk too.

The animals go into the van.

The animals are on the move.

They are going home!

12 o'clock

Picture Glossary

animals

farm

lamb

rabbits

chickens

goats

milk

sister